MINES AND BOOBY TRAPS

MILITARY TRAINING PAMPHLET No. 40

Part I (All Arms)—How to deal with individual mechanisms

1943

(This Pamphlet in conjunction with Part II supersedes Military Training Pamphlet No. 40, 1942)

The Naval & Military Press Ltd

Published by

The Naval & Military Press Ltd

Unit 5 Riverside, Brambleside
Bellbrook Industrial Estate
Uckfield, East Sussex
TN22 1QQ England

Tel: +44 (0)1825 749494

www.naval-military-press.com
www.nmarchive.com

*In reprinting in facsimile from the original, any imperfections are inevitably reproduced
and the quality may fall short of modern type and cartographic standards.*

ii

PREFATORY NOTE

1. Military Training Pamphlet No. 40, Mines and Booby Traps, will consist of the following parts :—

  Part I (All Arms)—How to deal with individual mechanisms.

  Part II (All Arms)—Laying and recording of British. mines.

  Part III (All Arms)—The breaching of minefields.

  Part IV—(In preparation).

2. The above-mentioned pamphlets should be studied by all commanders, i.e. battalion and upwards.

3. Blank pages are included in Part I for pasting in amendments which will be issued when new devices are taken into use.

DISTRIBUTION (Part I)

All arms   D
OCTUs   IV

CONTENTS

CHAPTER I
ALLIED MINES

MINES AND BOOBY TRAPS

MILITARY TRAINING PAMPHLET No. 40

GENERAL RULES

THESE SAVE LIVES. LEARN THEM LIKE YOUR ABC

1. If you **keep your eyes open** and suspect everything unusual, mines rapidly become merely a nuisance. It's only when you become **careless** that you are asking for **trouble.**

2. Look carefully all round a mine or booby trap **before** starting to work on it.

3. Handle all mines, fuzes, igniters and switches with **care at all times.**

4. **Never use force.** If a thing will not come undone gently by hand, leave it.

5. It generally takes **only one man** to work on a mine—**others keep off** and lie down.

6. **Look out for booby traps** (*see* next page).

7. Never pull a slack wire and never cut a taut one. Look at both ends of any wire before you touch it.

8. Safety-pin anti-personnel mines before you lift them.

9. If you have to leave a mine or trap unlifted **mark it obviously.**

10. If you find any mine or mechanism not described in this booklet, or anything you are not confident you understand, **leave it alone, mark it obviously** and inform the sappers.

11. **Don't** be fooled by the name "anti-tank" mine. It blows up anything on wheels just as well as it does a tank.

BOOBY TRAPS ON MINES

Mines laid by the enemy will normally be found buried, or with tops flush with the ground surface. They will frequently be **booby-trapped** to **catch** the **clumsy** and **incautious** lifter.

Traps will normally be in the form of another charge underneath the mine, set off by a pull igniter attached to the mine by a wire.

The **Tellermine** is designed for booby-trapping, but all mines can be booby-trapped.

Therefore **always suspect a booby trap.**

1. **Feel carefully all round and underneath** the mine for wires and igniters.

2. **Neutralize** each igniter as you come to it.

3. Examine both ends of any wire for igniters.

4. **Don't** lift mine until you are sure it is clear.

Note.—In special circumstances, when speed is vital, **pulling clear without searching for booby traps** may be ordered.

This order will **not** be given by anyone below Divisional Commander.

BRITISH MINE   MK V.

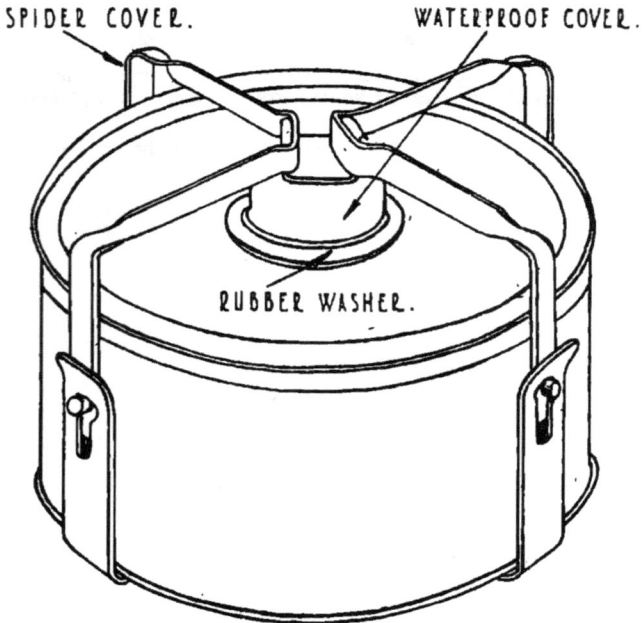

FUZE.

INSERT SAFETY PIN HERE.

SPIDER COVER.

WATERPROOF COVER.

RUBBER WASHER.

CHAPTER I

SECTION I.—ANTI-TANK MINE

BRITISH MK V

Size.—Circular/8 ins diameter, 4 ins high.

Weight.—About 12 lb (containing about 8 lb explosive).

Safety device.—Safety pin in the top of the fuze.

Description.—The fuze sits in a pocket in the centre of the top of the mine ; over it sits a tin cap on a rubber washer to keep moisture out of the fuze pocket. The fuze is operated by a spider frame which fits over the top of the mine and is held in place by studs which fit into slotted straps on the side of the mine.

To arm

  i. Check that the shear wire of fuze is not damaged (if it is—discard the fuze).
  ii. Put the fuze in the mine and remove the safety pin with a horizontal pull using pliers.
  iii. Place the rubber washer and tin cap over it and replace spider cover.

To disarm

  i. Remove cover without putting undue pressure on it.
  ii. Insert safety pin or nail or strong piece of wire in safety pin hole.
  iii. Remove fuze.

Note.—You may meet British Mk IV mines. They are similar to the Mk V but have an overall solid cover in place of the spider frame, and no waterproof cap.

BRITISH No75 GRENADE MINE. MK.I.

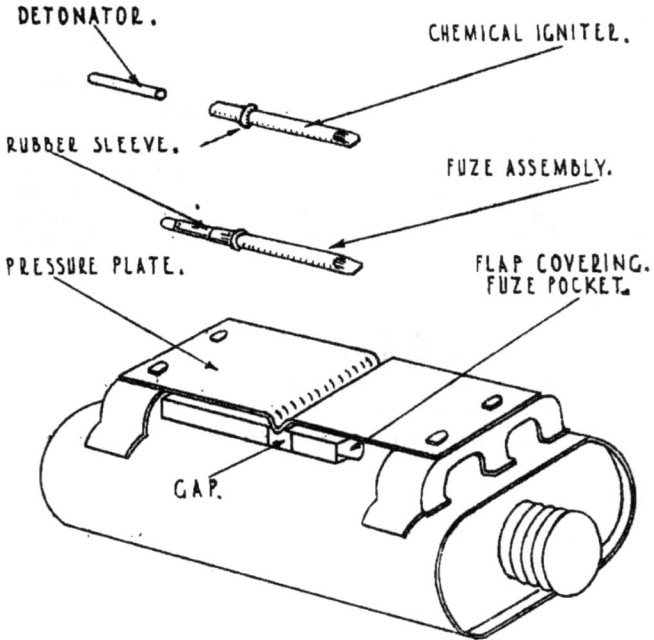

DETONATOR.

CHEMICAL IGNITER.

RUBBER SLEEVE.

FUZE ASSEMBLY.

PRESSURE PLATE.

FLAP COVERING.
FUZE POCKET.

GAP.

(MK II) IGNITER

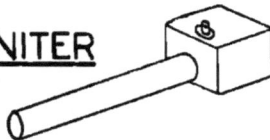

ANTI-TANK MINE

BRITISH No. 75 GRENADE MINE, MK 1

Size.—7 ins by 4 ins.

Weight.—About 3 lb (containing about $1\frac{1}{2}$ lb explosive).

Safety device.—Nil.

Description.—The mine is operated by the V-shaped indent on the pressure plate crushing the chemical igniters of the fuze.

To arm

i. Assemble the fuze by inserting detonator into igniter (putting the open ends together) and fasten with the rubber sleeve on the igniter.

ii. Insert a fuze into each of the two pockets under the pressure plate, pushing the detonator end in first, and ensure that the RED paint is visible in the gap.

iii. Close the flaps at the ends of the pockets to prevent the fuzes falling out.

To disarm

Open the flaps and remove both fuzes. The igniter and detonator must be taken apart and stored separately.

Note.—There is a Mk II edition of this mine with the following alterations :—

i. The fuze is in one piece and is operated by a pressure pin. (*See* sketch).

ii. The two pockets for the fuzes are inclined at an angle to allow for easier insertion.

AMERICAN MINE M.I.

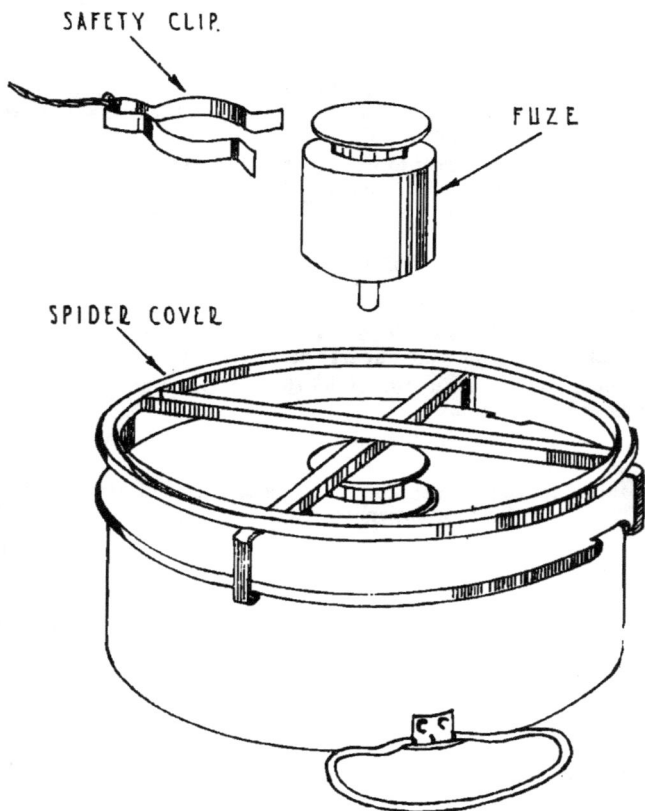

SAFETY CLIP.

FUZE

SPIDER COVER

ANTI-VEHICLE MINE

AMERICAN MK 1

Size.—Circular, 8 ins diameter and 4 ins high.

Weight.—About 10 lb (containing about 6 lb explosive).

Safety device.—Safety " bicycle " clip, which fits on fuze.

Description.—This mine is very similar to the British Mk V.

To arm

   i. Place fuze in fuze pocket.

  ii. Replace spider cover.

 iii. Remove safety " bicycle " clip.

To disarm

   i. Replace safety " bicycle " clip, or similar improvization.

  ii. Remove spider cover.

 iii. Remove fuze.

BRITISH SHRAPNEL MINE MK II

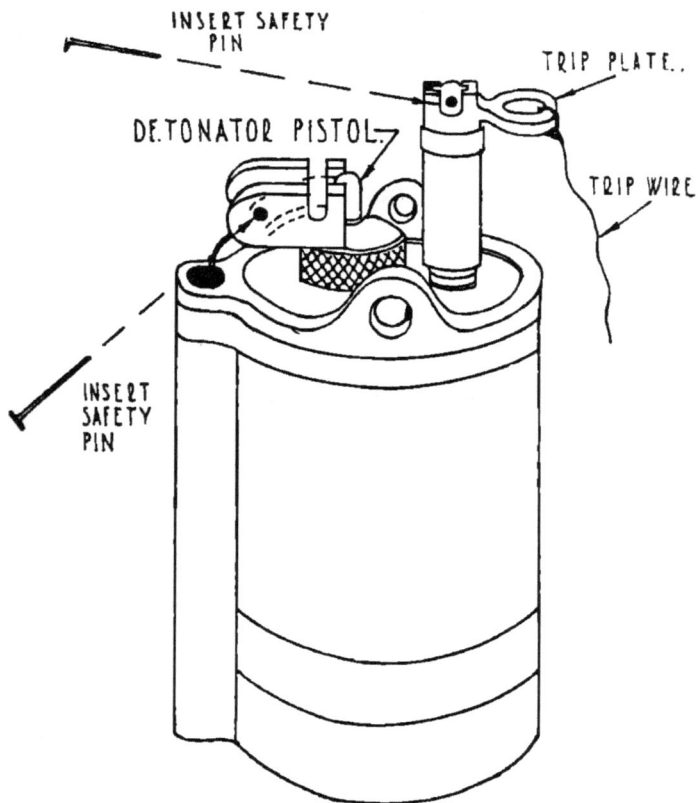

INSERT SAFETY PIN

TRIP PLATE.

DETONATOR PISTOL

TRIP WIRE

INSERT SAFETY PIN

SECTION 2.—ANTI-PERSONNEL MINE

BRITISH SHRAPNEL MINE, MK I

Size.—Cylindrical, about 6 ins high and 3 ins diameter.

Weight.—About 10 lb (containing about 1 lb of explosive).

Safety device.—TWO safety pins.

Description.—The mine is designed to jump a few feet in the air before bursting. Fragmentation of the thick casing produces the anti-personnel effect. It is set off by a trip wire. The mine has two projections on the top. The taller one is the " cartridge pistol " for projecting the mine into the air. The other one is the " detonator pistol " for exploding the mine in the air, and consists of a release mechanism similar to that on a mills bomb (Grenade 36 m).

The lever arm slides in a slot in the outer casing in which the mine sits.

To arm

  i. Ensure that BOTH pistols have SAFETY PINS IN PLACE.
  ii. Remove cartridge pistol (the larger projection) and inspect hole to see that it is clear.
  iii. Insert a cartridge and replace pistol, screwing up tight with tool provided.
  iv. Remove detonator pistol by turning knurled ring *clockwise* and inspect hole to see that it is clear.
  v. Insert a detonator, small end downwards. Shake gently to ensure the cap head rests on shoulder in the hole.
  vi. Replace detonator pistol with lever down the slot in the outer casing and screw up knurled ring *anti-clockwise*.
  vii. Check both safety pins.
  viii. Lay mine and attach trip wire to the trip plate on the top of the cartridge pistol. Too much tension will cause safety pin to jamb.
  ix. Remove safety pin of cartridge pistol.
  x. Remove safety pin of detonator pistol, being careful not to disturb the mine.

To neutralize

  i. Replace detonator pistol safety pin.
  ii. Replace cartridge pistol safety pin.
  iii. Cut trip wire.
  iv. Disarm mine by reversing procedure for arming and removing the detonator and cartridge.

MK II

Almost exactly the same, but the lever arm of the detonator pistol is longer.

AMERICAN MINE M2

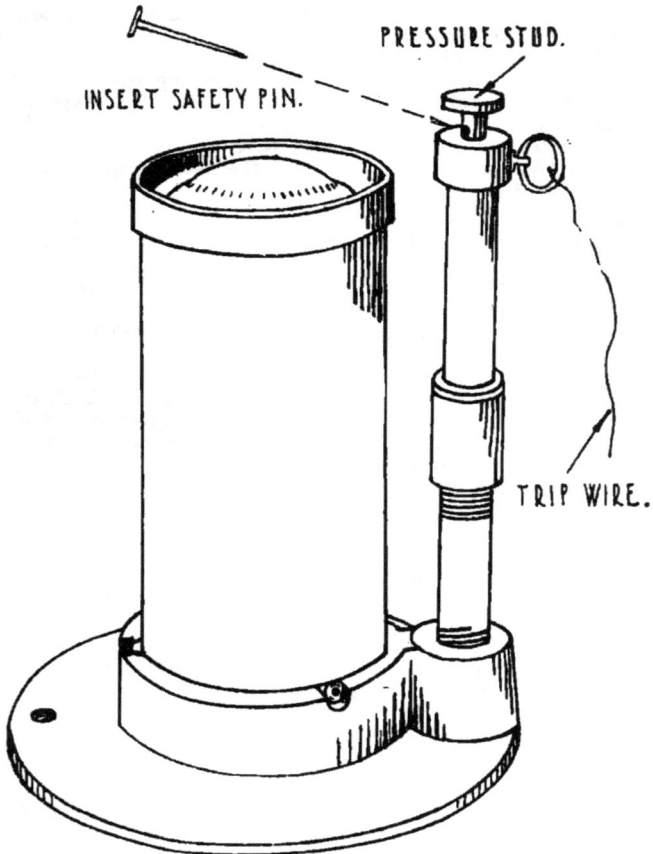

INSERT SAFETY PIN.

PRESSURE STUD.

TRIP WIRE.

ANTI-PERSONNEL MINE

AMERICAN MK 2

Size.—About 7 ins by 4 ins.

Weight.—About 8 lb (containing about 1 lb of explosive).

Safety device.—Safety pin in the igniter.

Description.—This mine is similar in action to the British Shrapnel mine.

The firing device can be operated either by pulling on a trip wire or by pressure on the knob.

To neutralize

    i. Place a nail or piece of strong wire in the safety pin hole in the igniter.

    ii. Cut the trip wire or remove pressure knob (whichever applies).

    iii. Unscrew the igniter.

BRITISH   RELEASE   SWITCH.

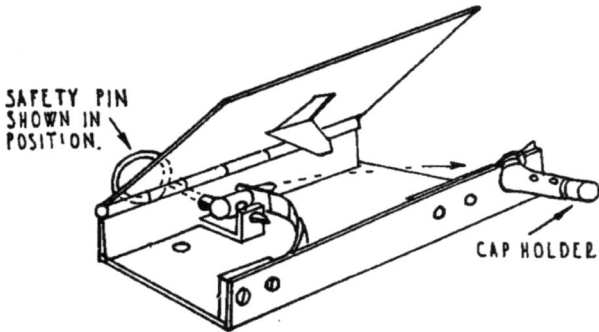

SAFETY PIN
SHOWN IN
POSITION.

CAP HOLDER

BRITISH   PRESS SWITCH.

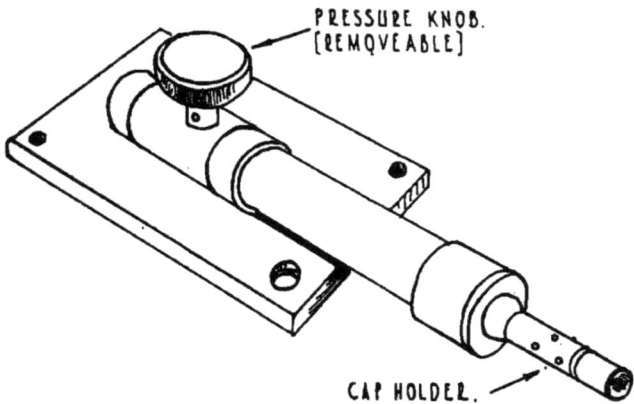

PRESSURE KNOB.
[REMOVEABLE]

CAP HOLDER.

SECTION 3.—BOOBY TRAP SWITCHES

British RELEASE switch

This operates rather like a book opening.

A tapered tongue projects inside the lid and bears against the spring when the switch is armed. The pressure of the spring tends to force the lid up. The lid is kept down by a weight—its removal will release the striker which fires a cap. Used under packing-cases and similar objects likely to be moved. Only a slight movement is necessary to fire it.

To disarm

   i. Insert a safety pin or nail or piece of strong wire in the hole. The pin MUST go through both casing and striker head (as in sketch).

   ii. Disconnect the cap holder.

Note.—If you cannot get at the switch to insert a safety pin you may be able to cut the fuze coming from it.

British PRESS switch

This switch is operated by pressure on the knob which releases a spring-loaded striker. It may be used under boards, mats, etc., and is fired by a weight of about 30 lb.

To disarm

   i. Remove the knob.

   ii. Disconnect the cap holder.

General note

Both these switches may be used with safety or instantaneous fuze.

BRITISH   IGNITERS.

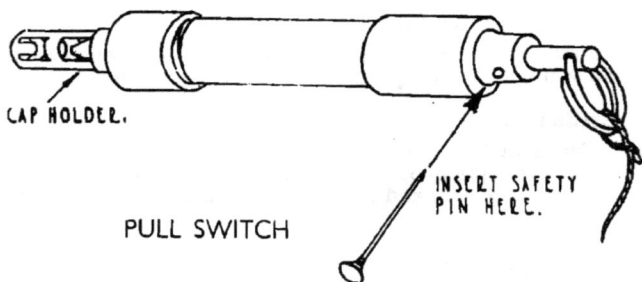

CAP HOLDER.

INSERT SAFETY
PIN HERE.

PULL SWITCH

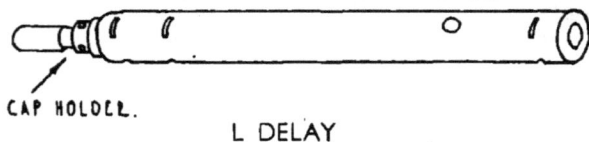

CAP HOLDER.

L DELAY

BOOBY TRAP SWITCHES

British PULL switch

This switch is used with a trip wire, which releases the striker when pulled.

To disarm

    i. Insert safety pin or nail or piece of strong wire in the hole.

    ii. Cut trip wire.

    iii. Disconnect the cap holder.

British L delay (lead break)

This igniter contains a spring-loaded striker, held back by a lead strip which stretches and eventually breaks under the action of the spring. Initially the striker is held in place by a safety pin.

There are various delays from 1 hour to 28 days. The igniter can be fitted direct to a detonator or safety fuze (using an adaptor).

To disarm

    i. It is no use trying to insert a safety pin as the striker will have moved.

    ii. There is no means of telling the delay remaining— therefore, gently remove by (a) cutting safety fuze, (b) if fitted to a detonator, by removal of igniter and detonator which should be put in a safe place. No attempt should be made to disconnect the detonator from the igniter.

General note

Both the pull switch and the L delay may be used with safety or instantaneous fuzes.

BRITISH PRESSURE/PULL SWITCH.
ELECTRIC.

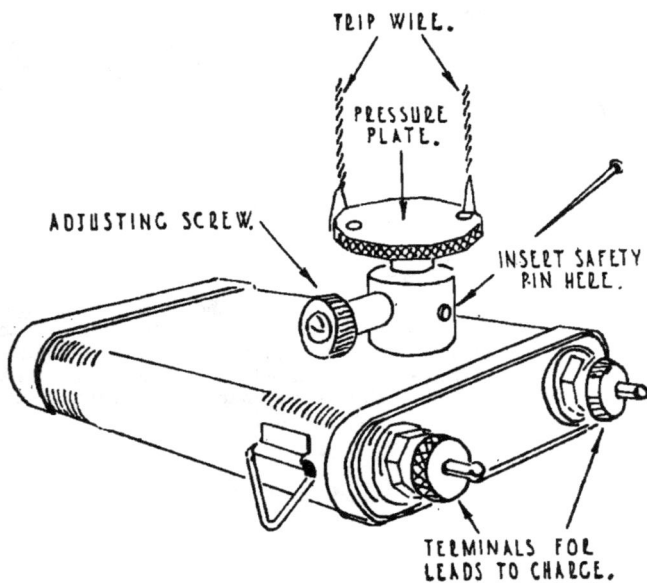

TRIP WIRE.

PRESSURE PLATE.

ADJUSTING SCREW.

INSERT SAFETY PIN HERE.

TERMINALS FOR LEADS TO CHARGE.

BOOBY TRAP SWITCHES

British PRESSURE/PULL Switch (Electric)

This switch contains a small battery and is designed to fire an electric detonator when either a trip wire is pulled *or* pressure is put on the plate. The pressure required to actuate the switch can be varied. The lightest pressure required is about 5 lb.

To neutralize

    i. Insert safety pin or nail or piece of strong wire in safety pin hole.

    ii. Disconnect leads.

AMERICAN RELEASE SWITCH M I.

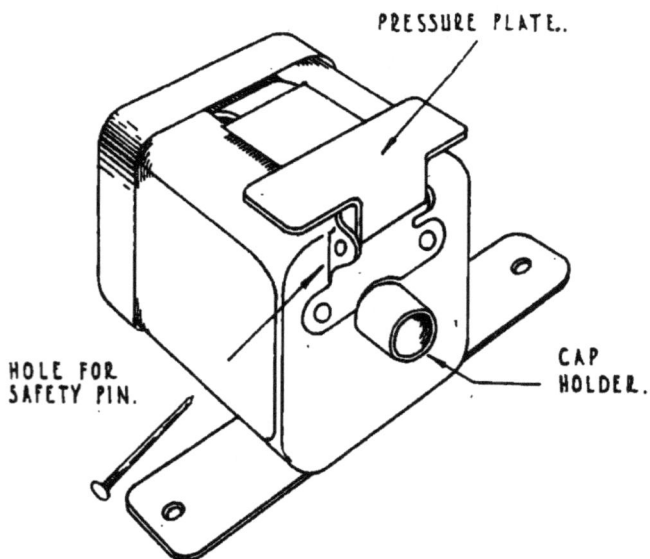

PRESSURE PLATE.

HOLE FOR
SAFETY PIN.

CAP
HOLDER.

BOOBY TRAP SWITCHES

American PULL switch, M1

This is essentially the same as the British pull switch, with one main modification : the cap holder is threaded to fit the American hand grenade and it can also be fitted to a detonator in addition to safety or instantaneous fuze.

To disarm.

i. Insert safety pin or nail or piece of strong wire in safety pin hole.

ii. Disconnect.

American PRESS switch, M1

This is essentially the same as the British press switch. The cap holder is the same as that used in the American pull switch (described above). The pressure knob is held by a small spring and can NOT be removed.

To disarm

Disconnect.

(Taking care NOT to exert pressure on the knob.)

American RELEASE switch, M1

The action is essentially the same as the British release switch, but its appearance differs. The cap holder is the same as described for the American PULL switch. When armed a pressure of at least 2 lb is required to hold down the release plate, which is normally held in position by a safety pin. (*See* sketch.)

To disarm

Replace safety pin or nail and disconnect.

GERMAN TELLERMINE 35 [No1.]

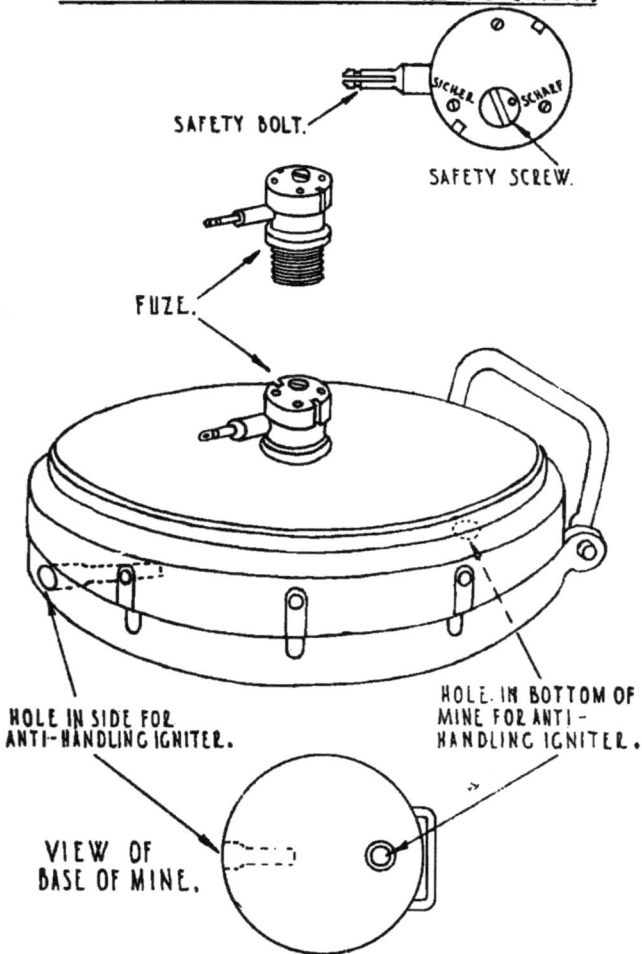

SAFETY BOLT.

SICHER SCHARF

SAFETY SCREW.

FUZE.

HOLE IN SIDE FOR
ANTI-HANDLING IGNITER.

HOLE IN BOTTOM OF
MINE FOR ANTI-
HANDLING IGNITER.

VIEW OF
BASE OF MINE.

CHAPTER II

SECTION 4.—ANTI-TANK MINE

GERMAN TELLERMINE 35 (No. 1)

Size.—Circular, about 13 ins diameter.

Weight.—About 20 lb (containing about 12 lb of explosive).

Safety device.—Safety bolt and safety screw in the fuze.

Description.—The mine has a dome-shaped cover plate in the centre of which is screwed a brass fuze.

Pressure on any part of the cover plate will fire the mine. It is fitted with a carrying handle.

Anti handling devices.—There are TWO holes in the body of the mine threaded to take the standard German igniters (described on pages 63, 65). These holes are situated :—

    i. One opposite the handle in the side of the mine.

    ii. One in the bottcm about half way between the handle and the centre of the mine.

Anti handling igniters when fitted are almost invariably pull igniters.

To neutralize

    (a) IF HAND LIFTING IS ORDERED .

      i. SEARCH FOR AND NEUTRALIZE BOOBY TRAPS which will almost certainly be present with this mine (see page 3).

      ii. Unscrew the main fuze.

      iii. Point the fuze away from you, and turn the screw so that the RED DOT is opposite the slot marked SICHER which may be coloured GREEN or WHITE.

      iv. Push home the safety bolt.

      v. Replace the fuze (which is now safe) in the mine.

      vi. Lift the mine and unscrew any anti-handling igniters.

      vii. Remove the detonators from the anti-handling holes.

(b) IF PULLING CLEAR WITHOUT SEARCHING FOR BOOBY TRAPS IS ORDERED

      i. Drop a loop on the end of about 50 yards of signal cable or strong cord over the fuze, or if you cannot do this, tie it to the handle. Do NOT move the mine or handle while doing this as it may be booby trapped.

      ii. Take cover at full length of the cable and pull the mine clear.

      iii. If the mine has not detonated, unscrew the main fuze and make it safe by carrying out iii and iv as for hand lifting.

      iv. Replace the fuze.

GERMAN   TELLERMINE 42 (No 2)

FUZE

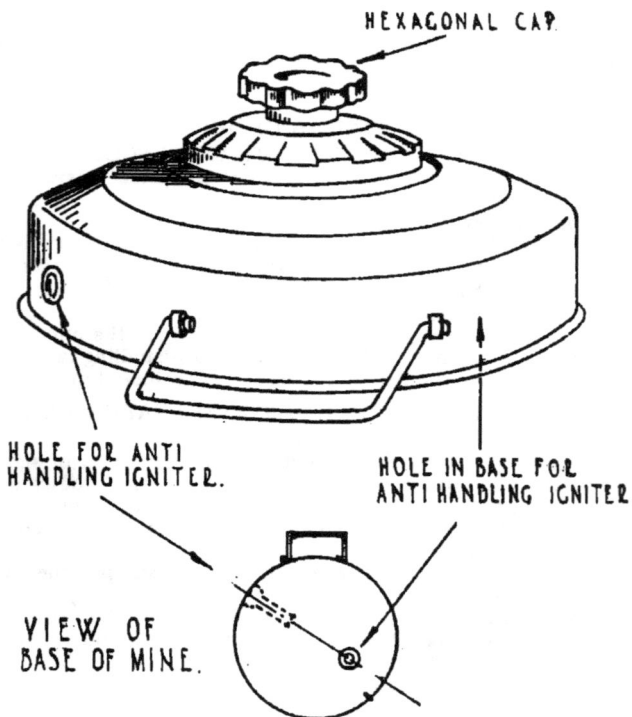

HEXAGONAL CAP.

HOLE FOR ANTI
HANDLING IGNITER.

HOLE IN BASE FOR
ANTI HANDLING IGNITER

VIEW OF
BASE OF MINE.

ANTI-TANK MINE
GERMAN TELLERMINE 42 (No. 2)

In general appearance this mine is similar to the Tellermine 35 (No. 1) with the following important differences :—

  i. *The fuze* is quite different. It is much smaller, has a detonator screwed on to the bottom of it, SLIDES into the fuze box and works on the same principle as our own Mk V mine fuze, but has no safety device.

    When in position a hexagonal cap screws over it into the cover.

  ii. *The holes for anti-handling igniters* are in a different position in relation to the handle. (*See* sketch.)

  iii. The pressure plate is fluted and extends over only about half of the top of the mine.

To neutralize

(*a*) IF HAND LIFTING IS ORDERED

  i. SEARCH FOR AND NEUTRALIZE BOOBY TRAPS which will almost certainly be present with this mine. (*See* page 3.)

  ii. Unscrew hexagonal cap.

  iii. Remove fuze and replace hexagonal cap.

  iv. Unscrew anti-handling igniters and remove detonators.

(*b*) IF PULLING CLEAR IS ORDERED

  i. Drop a loop on the end of about 50 yards of signal cable or strong cord over the fuze, or if you cannot do this, tie it to the handle. Do NOT move the mine or handle while doing this, as it may be booby trapped.

  ii. Take cover at full length of the cable and pull the mine clear.

  iii. If the mine has not detonated, unscrew hexagonal cap.

  iv. Remove fuze and replace hexagonal cap.

ANTI-TANK MINE
GERMAN TELLERMINE No. 3

This mine is really the Tellermine No. 1 with a fluted cover plate. It may also be found with a Tellermine No. 2 type fuze, in which case a screwed plug with a milled head screws into the hole in the cover plate over the fuze in the same way as the hexagonal cap in the Tellermine No. 2.

To neutralize

Follow the instructions for Tellermine No. 1 or 2 according to the type of fuze.

FRENCH LIGHT ANTI-TANK MINE

FUZE.

FILLING PLUG

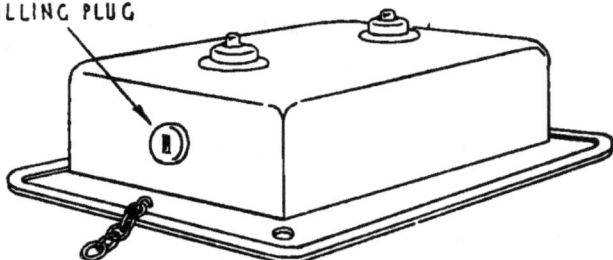

MINE WITHOUT LID.

HOLE FOR
SAFETY BAR.

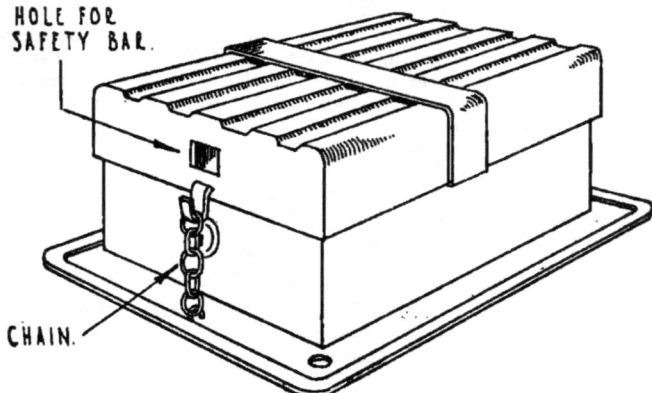

CHAIN.

MINE COMPLETE.

ANTI-TANK MINE

FRENCH LIGHT ANTI-TANK MINE

Size.—12 ins long by 9 ins wide by 5 ins high.

Weight.—About 12 lb (containing about 6 lb of explosive).

Safety device.—None in the fuze.

A safety bar can be slipped in between the fuzes and the lid.

Description.—The mine consists of a rectangular box with a corrugated cover, which is held down on to the mine by a chain at each end.

Two fuzes of similar type to our Mk 5 fuze screw into the mine under the lid.

To neutralize

(a) IF HAND LIFTING IS ORDERED

  i. SEARCH FOR AND NEUTRALIZE BOOBY TRAPS. (*See* page 3.)

  ii. Carefully remove chain from one end and without exerting pressure lift the lid.

  iii. Unscrew and remove fuzes, taking care not to press on the centre of the striker heads.

  iv. Handle the fuze with care after removal as the detonator is still fixed to it. Accidents have occurred through careless handling after removal.

(b) IF PULLING CLEAR WITHOUT SEARCHING FOR BOOBY TRAPS IS ORDERED

  i. Carefully attach a 50 yard length of signal cable to the mine and pull clear.

  ii. If the mine has not detonated carry out operations ii, iii, and iv for hand lifting.

HUNGARIAN MINE C.V.P.I.

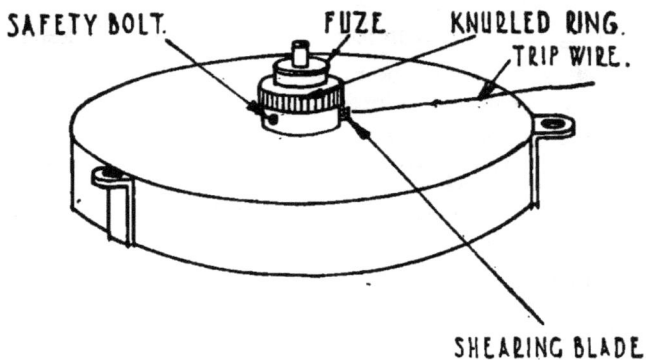

SAFETY BOLT. FUZE KNURLED RING.
TRIP WIRE.

SHEARING BLADE

MINE WITHOUT COVER.

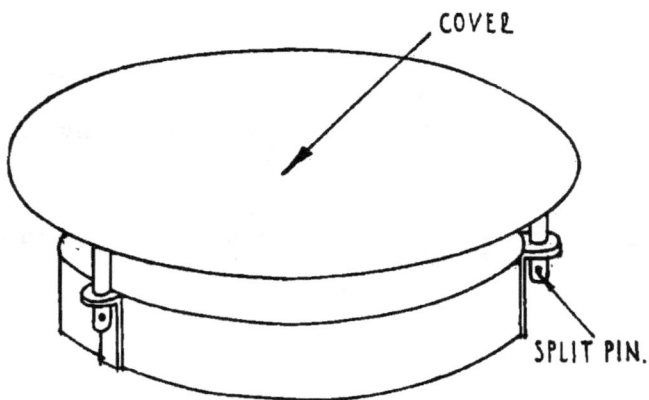

COVER

SPLIT PIN.

MINE COMPLETE.

ANTI-TANK MINE

HUNGARIAN C.V.P.1

This mine may also be set as an anti-PERSONNEL mine

Size.—Circular about 8 ins diameter and 3 ins high.

Weight.—About 8 lb (containing about 4 lb. of explosive).

Safety device.—A hole in the side of the fuze to take a safety bolt.

Description.—The mine has a cover, which acts as a pressure plate, sitting on top of the fuze which screws into the body of the mine. Attached to the pressure plate are three vertical legs which slide in brackets attached to the body, and may be held down by split pins through the legs under the brackets. The fuze can be adjusted to fire at varying pressures, giving an anti-TANK mine or an anti-PERSONNEL mine fired by pressure or a trip wire.

To disarm

As this mine may be set to go off at light pressure, BE CAREFUL.

  (a) IF LIFTING BY HAND IS ORDERED

   i. If there is a trip wire from the fuze—cut it.

   ii. SEARCH FOR AND NEUTRALIZE BOOBY TRAPS (*See* page 3).

   iii. Free the cover plate.

   iv. Lift off the cover plate CAREFULLY.

   v. Insert a large nail into the safety bolt hole.

   vi. Unscrew fuze CAREFULLY WITHOUT touching the knurled ring.

  (b) IF PULLING CLEAR WITHOUT SEARCHING FOR BOOBY TRAPS IS ORDERED.

   i. If there is a TRIP WIRE, put a loop of 50 yards of signal cable round the trip wire, take cover, and pull.

   ii. If there is no trip wire put a loop of 50 yards of signal cable round the legs, take cover and pull clear.

   iii. If the mine has not detonated carry out operations iii, iv, v and vi as for hand lifting.

ITALIAN MINE
B.2

DO <u>NOT</u>
TOUCH THIS.

REMOVE THIS!

REMOVE CAP
HOLDER.

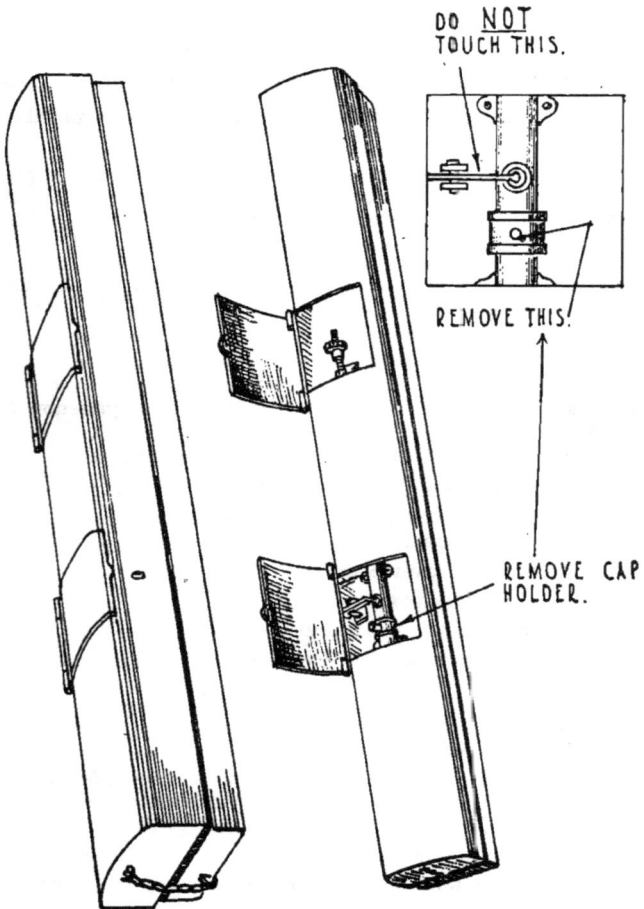

ANTI-TANK MINE

ITALIAN B2

Size.—3 ft 6 ins by 5 ins by 5 ins.

Weight.—About 33 lb (containing about 7 lb of explosive).

Safety device.—A removable cap holder.

Description.—The mine is a rectangular metal box, with an overall cover attached by chains at each end. There are two inspection lids in the cover. The charge is placed in both ends of the box. The firing mechanism is in the middle. The striker is held clear of the cap by a wire, which is sheared by a knife edge on the underside of the lid when it is pressed down.

To disarm

(a) IF LIFTING BY HAND IS ORDERED

  i. SEARCH FOR AND NEUTRALIZE BOOBY TRAPS (*See* page 3.)

  ii. Open both inspection lids carefully.

  iii. Remove CAP HOLDER CAREFULLY (*see* inset sketch) and DO NOT TOUCH THE LEVER.

(b) IF PULLING CLEAR WITHOUT SEARCHING FOR BOOBY TRAPS IS ORDERED

  i. Pull clear with 50 yards of cable.

  ii. Carry out ii and iii as for hand lifting, if mine is still there.

GERMAN 'S' MINE

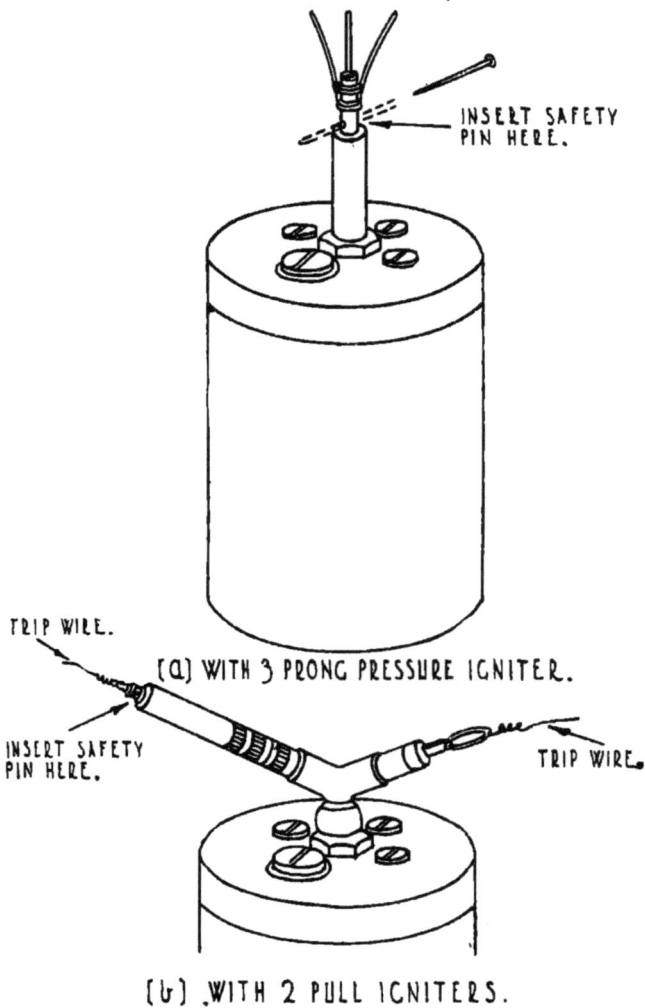

INSERT SAFETY
PIN HERE.

TRIP WIRE.

(a) WITH 3 PRONG PRESSURE IGNITER.

INSERT SAFETY
PIN HERE.

TRIP WIRE.

(b) WITH 2 PULL IGNITERS.

SECTION 5.—ANTI-PERSONNEL MINE

GERMAN S MINE

This is a small cylindrical mine about 4 ins diameter and 5 ins high. On firing, the mine is projected about 3 ft into the air where it explodes, scattering steel balls in all directions. It is purely an anti-PERSONNEL mine. Up to date there are three normal methods of operation.

1. THE MOST COMMON method is using the *standard 3-prong pressure* igniter (*see* page 63).

To neutralize

Insert nail into safety pin hole and unscrew igniter.

2. ANOTHER METHOD *is using one or two standard pull igniters*. An adaptor is used when pull igniters are fitted (*see* page 65).

To neutralize

  i. Insert nail, etc., in safety pin hole and cut trip wires.

  ii. Unscrew igniters.

  iii. Inspect other end of all trip wires for other " S " mines or booby traps.

3. ANOTHER METHOD *is using the* 3-*prong pressure igniters* (*electric*) (*see* page 67).

To neutralize

Carefully trace the leads to the mine and cut all leads coming from it.

ITALIAN   MINE   B.4.

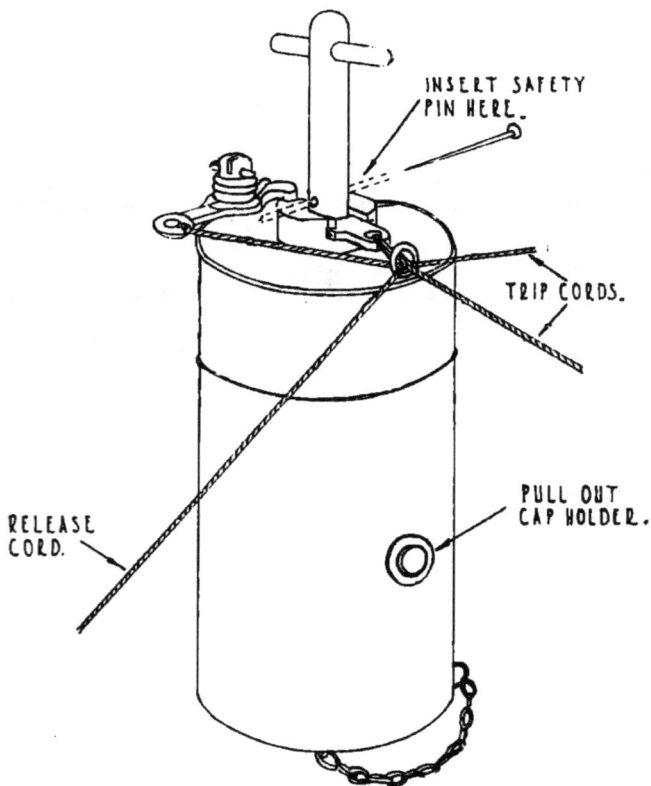

INSERT SAFETY
PIN HERE.

TRIP CORDS.

PULL OUT
CAP HOLDER.

RELEASE
CORD.

ANTI-PERSONNEL MINE

ITALIAN B4

This is a shrapnel mine and on discharge scatters scrap metal. It is usually fixed above the ground to a tree or post as it has no " jack-in-the-box " effect like the British and German types, but has been used buried. It is fired by pulling a trip wire or by cutting a tension wire.

To neutralize

    i. Withdraw cap holder.

    ii. Insert stout wire or nail in safety pin hole in striker.

    iii. Release cords, checking other ends for booby traps.

GERMAN PULL IGNITER
ZDSCHN ANZ 29 (FRICTION).

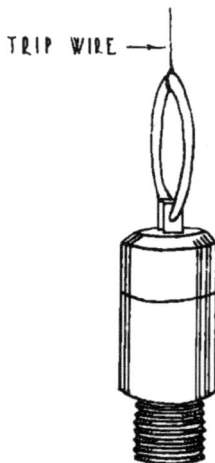

TRIP WIRE →

GERMAN PULL IGNITER ZZ.35.

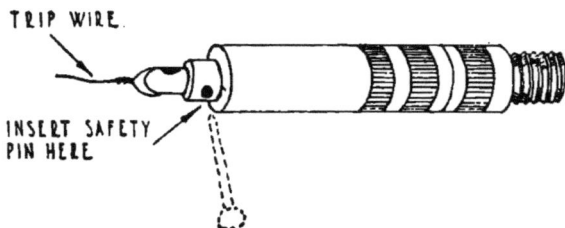

TRIP WIRE.

INSERT SAFETY
PIN HERE

GERMAN IGNITERS

(FOR MINES OR BOOBY TRAPS)

German pull igniter (friction) ZDSCHN ANZ29

This igniter can be recognized by the large ring attached to the end, and may be found with " S " mines and in booby traps.

To neutralize

Cut wire carefully and unscrew igniter.

N.B.—This igniter has no safety pin.

German pull igniter ZZ35

Action is very similar to our pull switch and it is used with trip wire in the same way. Used with " S " mines either singly or in pairs, and in booby traps.

To neutralize

    i. Place a nail or strong wire in the safety pin hole.

    ii. Unscrew.

GERMAN 3 PRONG PRESSURE IGNITER.

ELECTRIC TYPE.

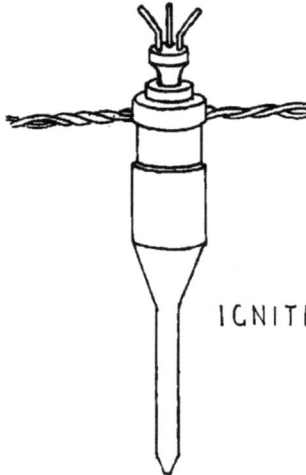

IGNITER.

CUT LEADS HERE.

CUT LEAD HERE.

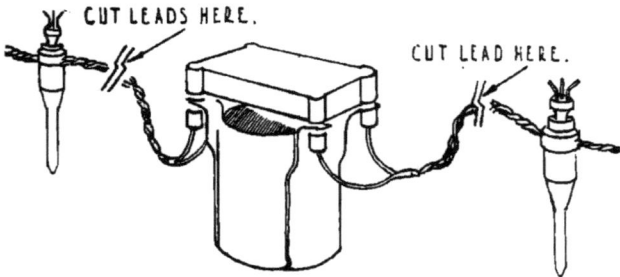

S. MINE.
FITTED FOR USE WITH THIS IGNITER.

GERMAN IGNITERS

(FOR MINES OR BOOBY TRAPS)

German 3-prong pressure igniter (electric), ES Mi Z40

Used with the " S " mine this is a variation of the standard
3-prong pressure igniter, which fires an electric detonator in
the mine. This set up is usually found with one mine
operated by any of 18 igniters used in two chains of 9, thus
increasing the radius of action of the mine.

To neutralize

Trace leads to mine and cut all leads coming from mine.

TRAINING MANUALS, TEXT BOOKS AND INSTRUCTIONS

The backbone of all successful armies is its training and tactics. The Naval and Military Press publishes many such manuals of instruction – all perviously long out of print . So, whether your interest lies in the infantry and cavalry tactics of the earliest regiments of the British army in the 18th century, or the weapons manuals and firing instructions of 20th century warfare, the Naval and Military Press has the right book for you.

www.naval-military-press.com

MINES AND BOOBY TRAPS 1943

This is a War Office pamphlet, issued mid-war, in 1943. Its purpose is to

introduce sappers to mines commonly used by the British Army – and how to deal with similar devices set by the Germans. The devices described and illustrated cover British anti-tank; grenade; shrapnel and assorted booby trap switches. Enemy mines are covered in chapter 2 with anti-tank, Teller mine types; French anti-tank; Hungarian; anti-personnel German and Italian; and igniters.This is a concise but comprehensive guide for British Army sappers in the art of demining or mine clearance.
9781474539395

THE .303 LEWIS GUN

Illustrated with good clear line drawings this 1941 weapon guide tells

the Home Guard Volunteer how to use the 303 Lewis Gun effectively against the invading enemy.A reprint of an original handbook for the .303 Lewis Gun, that was first published in 1941. This book is a practical guide to the handling and maintenance of this iconic weapon.In the crisis following the Fall of France, where a large part of the British Army's equipment had been lost up to and at Dunkirk, stocks of Lewis guns in both .303 and .30-06 were hurriedly pressed back into service, primarily for Home Guard use. Full of fascinating information, this book taught the user the guns capabilities and all he needed to know about maintenance and combat use. Number 2 in the wartime Nicholson & Watson "Know Your Weapons" series, that offer all the important information in a more vivid style than an official publication. Illustrated with good clear line drawings.
9781474539456

ANTI-TANK WEAPONS

Smash The Tank

An insight into the amateur side of World War 2. Diagrams illustrate the

main points and the devices, such as the Thermos Bomb;Phosrhorus Bomb;Sticky Bombs; that could be cobbled together from household items are described.This pamphlet was available to the Home Guard and describes the German tank and how to destroy it. It is an early War publication c1940, dealing with the light tanks used by the Germans, also the author gives examples of anti-tank actions in the Spanish Civil War, in which he took part. I'ts is a fascinating look at the "enthusiastic" approach to killing tanks.

9781474539449

TANK HUNTING AND DESTRUCTION 1940

The stated object for the distributing of this War Office manual was as "A

guide and help to troops who have the determination and nerve to destroy tanks at close quarters". Intended for fighting on home soil after the very real possibility of a full German invasion, "Operation Sea Lion", this is a remarkable if somewhat naive snap shot of Britain state of preparedness,in her most dangerous hour.

The contents details Tank hunting, Tank characteristics,Tactical

action,Road blocks,ambushes Ect,also includes an interesting appendix on Molotov Cocktails, and materials on other ways to destroy tanks.

9781474539401

TROOP TRAINING FOR LIGHT TANK TROOPS NOVEMBER 1939

Very early War tactics pertaining to various aspects of training with and

employing armour in the British Army. Covering in concise detail that which a Light tank crew needed to know to be effective in action.

In the early years of the war, Germany held the initiative. German forces

used Blitzkrieg tactics in France in 1940, making full use of the speed and armour of tanks to break through enemy defences. It was clear that German tank tactics had evolved during the inter-war period. By contrast, Britain and the Allies were playing catch-up.

9781474539302

JAPANESE WEAPONS ILLUSTRATED
September 1944

This period 'Restricted' laced binding manual was intended to be an aid

to the identification of Japanese Army equipment, with sections covering: Tanks, both two-man, Tankette, light and medium; Armoured Cars; Self-Propelled Guns; Anti-Tank Guns; Artillery; Anti-Aircraft Guns; Mortars & Grenade Dischargers; Small Arms; Flamethrowers etc. Produced one year before the surrender of Japan, this work gives a good overview of the weapons the allies would find, fighting an army that despite being on the back foot, was still capable of stiff resistance in an almost entirely defensive role..
9781474539432

NOTES ON THE GERMAN ARMY-WAR
December 1940

An early war 393-page 'Notes' periodical manual from December 1940. It

is a detailed review, for use in the field. The manual looks at every aspect of the "Blitzkrieg" German Army (and, to some extent, the Air Force) and gives details as known at the time.

It covers the fighting arms and the services behind them – tactics,

organisation, weapons and equipment. It usefully also includes a colour section on uniforms and insignia, a black-and-white plate section of small arms, infantry support and anti-tank weapons, artillery and AFVs. A series of pull-outs related to the text covering tanks etc. are also reproduced.

This is an important first-class picture of the complex fighting machine

that was the German Army at the end of the campaigns of 1940, only six months before the invasion of Russia.
9781474539203

GERMAN MINES AND TRAPS
Mid-1940 War Office manual with details of German mines, both the Teller and S-mine (Bouncing Betty) are covered, with techniques for disarming. Good clear full-page line drawings give both practical and technical information. Highly recommended because of the illustrations, which show how these devices worked and the components.
9781474535809⊠

NOTES ON ENEMY ARMY IDENTIFICATIONS ITALY
October 1941

This period handbook was published to give British military personnel a

better understanding of the principal characteristics of both the Italian
army and the Black Shirt Militia under active service conditions , it is
dated October 1941.

It begins with a description of distinctive branches, or specialities, the

most characteristic of which was the arm of the Royal Carabinieri, a
semi-military body occupying, historically, the senior position in the
Army. Other specialities included the Grenadiers of Sardinia, the
Bersaglieri, the Alpini and the San Marco Marine Regiment
The handbook then goes on to show, in order, the organisation of
Command and Staff, of formations (corps and divisions) and of the arms
and services; services, supply and transportation; ranks, plates (many in
colour) cover uniforms, insignia, medals and decorations; armament and
equipment and a chapter on the Air Force, There are chapters on tactical
doctrine and principles of employment, on permanent fortifications,
camouflage and abbreviations. Finally there is a brief index.
9781474539746

MANUAL OF GUERILLA TACTICS
Specially Prepared And Based On Lessons From The Spanish And
Russian Campaigns

One of the excellent, concise Bernards Pocket Books, intended to show

members of the Home Guard and the regular forces that war is not
conducted in a gentlemanly way – it is kill or be killed.
9781474539463

THE OFFENSIVE OF SMALL UNITS
September 1916

This is a periodical tactical manual from 1916, it focuses on the manner

in which the French organised and executed their attacks and
counterattacks . Summarised from the French, it lays out the process by
which to operate in attacks on the German trenches. Focused purely on
the operation of infantry, the purpose of this British translation is to give
small infantry units the benefit of the French experience in regard to the
best methods of combat, in offensive operations.
9781474537971

TRENCH WARFARE
Notes on attack and defence, February 1915

This important period manual was published in early 1915 when hope of

a quick ending to the war disappeared, and trench warfare had begun to dominate the Western Front.

The manual strives to instil an offensive spirit and gives practical

examples on: Close quarter, local, methods of successful warfare, and German attacks. The salient points to gather were preparation and co-operation between artillery and infantry, and that the capture of trenches is easier than their retention. Two plates illustrating tactics complete this official publication.

9781474539807

Ministry Of Home Security
OBJECTS DROPPED FROM THE AIR 1941

An illustrated Official and confidential publication, covering the many

and varied types of objects that were falling from principally German aircraft during the Second phase of the blitz, including high explosives,incendiary bombs and small arms ammunition. Complete with 8 page addendum.

9781783319541

THE MUSKETRY INSTRUCTIONS FOR THE GERMAN INFANTRY 1887
(Schiessvorshrift fur die Infanterie) Translated for the intelligence Division War Office

Translated for the War Office by Colonel C W Bowdler Bell

A facsimile that includes the supplement for the German Infantry for

1887. Musketry exercises were intended to give the infantry instruction in shooting, to make effective use of their firearm in battle. As such the manual shows important details designed to make the infantry soldier battle-ready by the end of his first year of service. Instruction is subdivided into Preparatory exercises; Target practice; Field firing; Instructional firing; Inspection in musketry; Proving the rifle M/61.84 and revolver M/83. Many black powder weapons were still used, mainly for training purposes, up to end of the First World War.

9781783313631

(18758) G.173 400,000 5/43 K.II.K. Gp. 8/7